NAM

The Vietnam War

The War and U.S. Society

Published by Brown Bear Books Ltd

4877 N. Circulo Bujia
Tucson, AZ 85718
USA

and

First Floor
9-17 St. Albans Place
London N1 0NX

© 2013 Brown Bear Books Ltd

ISBN: 978-1-78121-045-1

Library of Congress Cataloging-in-Publication Data
available upon request

Editorial Director: Lindsey Lowe
Managing Editor: Tim Cooke
Design Manager: Keith Davis
Designer: Lynne Lennon
Picture Manager: Sophie Mortimer
Children's Publisher: Anne O'Daly
Production Director: Alastair Gourlay

Manufactured in the United States of America

CPSIA compliance information: Batch# AG/5506

Picture Credits
Front Cover: TopFoto: Charles Gatewood/The
Image Works main.

All photographs U.S. National Archives except:
Corbis: Angel Zayas/Demotix 38/39, Bettmann 43,
Chester Sheard–KPA/ZUMA 9, UIP 27; **Library of
Congress:** 38, 40, 41, 42; **Robert Hunt Library:**
5b, 10, 11, 13t, 21, 22/23; **TopFoto:** Alinari 7, 8,
Charles Gatewood/The Image Works 24.

Brown Bear Books Ltd. has made every effort to contact the
copyright holder. If you have any information please email
smortimer@windmillbooks.co.uk

All other photographs and artworks © Brown Bear Books Ltd.

Publisher's Note
Our editors have carefully reviewed the websites that appear
on page 47 to ensure that they are suitable for students. Many
websites change frequently, however, and we cannot guarantee
that a site's future contents will continue to meet our high
standards of quality. Be advised that students should be closely
supervised whenever they access the Internet.

Contents

INTRODUCTION

American ground forces served in Vietnam from 1965 to 1973. During that time, all the fighting occurred some 8,000 miles away from the United States. Americans at home were never under threat from attack. Nevertheless, the conflict dominated life in the United States for nearly a decade, and its repercussions still echo in public life. In the 2000 presidential election, for example, there were clashes about the Vietnam war record of both candidates, Al Gore and the eventual winner, George W. Bush. In 2008 Vietnam was again in the spotlight: the defeated Republican presidential candidate was the war hero John McCain.

Domestic impact of the war

For many Americans, the idea of U.S. military involvement in Vietnam was not originally as unpopular as it later became. Americans saw themselves as the protectors of the free world in the face of a threat from Communism, as spread by the Soviet Union and its allies and by China. U.S. industrial and military strength had played a decisive role in victory over the forces of fascism in World War II (1939–1945). When U.S. leaders warned of terrible consequences if South Vietnam was allowed to become Communist, many people supported their determination to stop the spread of Communism.

Once the fighting began, however, rifts soon opened up in U.S. society. It quickly became clear that the easy victory some people had naively hoped for would not be achieved. The war began to impact not only the economy, but also many thousands of families and communities whose young men were being asked to fight—and die—in a distant land for a cause that seemed to many people unclear.

The burden of the war, moreover, was clearly being disproportionately borne by the young, the poor, and the black, who were most liable to be drafted into the military. Protests against the war were originally led by

▼ U.S. Marines engage the enemy in 1966. The recruitment and equipping of such men had a profound impact on U.S. society.

small groups of radical students. Over time, however, they also attracted more moderate members of "mainstream" society disturbed by the impact of the war.

Political confusion

The Democratic Party had begun combat operations in Vietnam, and in the 1968 presidential election they paid the price. The new Republican president, Richard M. Nixon, promised to end the war. In fact, as people soon learned, he was secretly escalating a bombing campaign in Laos and Cambodia. There were further revelations in the so-called Pentagon Papers of 1971 that for a decade the government had repeatedly deceived the public about the conduct of the war.

Many people were confused. Americans had thought of themselves as the "good guys." Now it seemed that there were no good guys. The shock of that realization still reverberates through society today, where many people no longer trust the government and fear involvement in foreign affairs.

BURN DRAFT CARDS - NOT HILDREN

◀ Protestors demonstrate against U.S. military policy in New York in 1965. By that time, opposition to the war was growing.

Chapter 1

Recruitment and the Draft

As U.S. involvement in the war grew, so the recruitment of troops through conscription became the subject of bitter controversy.

◄ A new recruit has his Afro hairstyle shaved off on joining the armed services in the late 1960s.

When the Vietnam War started, the United States possessed the world's largest armed force. It had proved itself during World War II (1939–1945). In the Korean War (1950–1953) it had led the United Nations force fighting the Communist North Koreans and their Chinese allies. The armed services remained on high alert in the late 1950s and early 1960s. This was the time of the Cold War. The world was divided into two bitterly opposed camps. One was led by the United States and its allies; the other was led by the Communist Soviet Union. Hostilities seemed to be a constant threat.

When Vietnam rose up against its French colonial rulers and then dissolved into a civil war, the United States never intended that its armed forces would become fully involved

▲ Young soldiers pose for the camera soon after their arrival in Vietnam. The average age of U.S. combat troops was 19 years.

in the unfolding conflict. The government saw the role of the armed forces as being limited from the beginning, in part because public opinion would protest at a full-scale deployment. As a result, the United States never committed as many troops as would have been necessary to win the war in Vietnam—and yet it was gradually drawn into sending huge numbers of combat troops, even though they did not intend to try to win the war. Their role was to maintain the balance between North and South Vietnam. At the beginning of President John F. Kennedy's term in office in January 1961, there were 650 U.S. advisors in Vietnam, helping to train the troops of South Vietnam's Army of the Republic of Vietnam (ARVN). By the time of Kennedy's assassination in November 1963, there were 16,700 U.S. troops in the country. In 1968 the total reached a peak of nearly 550,000.

Spiraling war

Even when the United States became fully committed to the war in Vietnam in 1965, the use of armed force remained limited. U.S. involvement was largely intended to prevent the war from spreading. Throughout the conflict, U.S. troops were not permitted to escalate the fighting by invading neighboring North Vietnam, Laos, or Cambodia, even when there were operational reasons to do

▼ Recruits to the U.S. Army are dropped by helicopter during a training exercise.

KEY THEMES

Draft Dodgers

As the war escalated and casualties mounted, Americans became increasingly reluctant to be drafted. Some burned their draft cards, refused the induction, demonstrated, or fled to Canada. The boxer Muhammad Ali refused the draft and went to court to defend his viewpoint. Others found a legal way to avoid serving in Vietnam, such as joining the National Guard, continuing their studies, or faking a medical deferment. The large numbers of draft evaders remains the subject of bitter controversy.

so. (Instead, U.S. forces would take part in secret operations in all three countries.) They were also severely limited in their use of airpower, despite having virtual control of the skies from early in the conflict. U.S. forces deliberately did not attack certain targets in North Vietnam, for example, for fear of angering the Soviet Union and the Chinese. In all, the Communist forces only faced a small part of the potential military might of the United States. Yet despite such restrictions, and politically imposed limits on the number of military personnel sent to fight the war, thousands of ordinary young Americans found themselves conscripted to serve in a war in a far-away country they knew nothing about.

The draft

When Kennedy became president in 1961, the United States had a draft system that dated back to 1940 and World War II. All male citizens were required to register for the draft when they turned 18. They remained liable to be called up for two years' training and service at any time until they reached the age of 26. There had been complaints that the system needed to be reformed or abolished. Most such comments came from from the Republican Party. But most people were happy with the draft. They saw it as a necessary evil for a country that saw itself as having a duty to "bear the torch of freedom," as President Kennedy had expressed it in his inauguration speech.

▲ The burning of draft cards was initially a shocking gesture for many people, but later became more accepted.

One reason for the general acceptance of the draft was that the number of men recruited by the draft had been falling steadily since the end of the Korean War in 1953 as the requirements of the military declined. In 1953, 472,000 draftees were drafted. By 1960 the number had fallen to just 87,000. In 1963 a bill to renew the draft was passed by Congress without opposition.

In 1965, Kennedy's successor, President Lyndon B. Johnson, ordered the doubling of draft call-ups as he committed increased U.S. forces to Vietnam. Even now, polls suggested that two-thirds of high-school

▲ Young Marines enjoy pineapples. For many new recruits, deployment to Vietnam was the first time they had left the United States.

young man stood the same chance of having his name picked for service. In fact, however, that was not true.

students supported the draft, despite being the individuals most likely to be affected by it. Not everyone supported the draft, however. The Republican nominee for the 1964 presidential election, Barry Goldwater, called for the system to end. Opposition to the draft became widespread. By the end of the 1960s, it appeared to some people that only the U.S. Army itself still supported the draft.

The reason for the growing unpopularity of the draft was that it was widely seen as being unfair. The whole point of a draft was that the burden of military service was supposed to fall on everyone equally. In principle, any

Questions of fairness

The draft was officially termed the "Selective Service System." The "selective" part of the process went against the idea that the draft applied equally to all social classes and ethnic groups. In particular, certain groups were allowed to delay or escape their armed service with so-called deferments. The main people who benefited were college students and married men with children. They tended to be better-educated, middle-class young men. The burden of the draft tended to fall upon the poorly educated and the poor. In particular, a disproportionate amount of

▶ When John F. Kennedy became president in 1961, he followed the policy of President Dwight D. Eisenhower of supporting South Vietnam.

draftees were young black men from poor backgrounds.

The question of the fairness of the draft came to dominate public opinion. Despite the attention the draft attracted, however, only 25 percent of the six million men and women who served during the war were draftees. The others were volunteer servicemen and women.

Selection criteria were not the only reason to question the fairness of the draft. As the war dragged on, regular soldiers tended to face far less danger from enemy fire than the draftees. The infantry units in which the draftees served tended to be in more dangerous locations or on more risky missions than regular formations. In 1965, fewer than one-third of U.S. casualties were draftees. By 1969, the proportion had changed dramatically. At that time, draftees made up 16 percent of the armed forces in Vietnam, largely because they were only conscripted into the U.S. Army, not the other services. But they made up 88 percent of the infantry and accounted for nearly two-thirds of battle deaths. Such figures made it appear that the draftees were paying with their lives at a disproportionate rate. For many people, that underlined the injustice of the system.

Demonstrations and evasion

As the war became more unpopular, protests against the draft increased. The most popular form of protest was the burning of draft cards, sent to draftees at the start of their service. In the early days of draft-card burning, most people were offended by what they saw as an unpatriotic act. But as the war continued, it became more accepted as a form of protest.

As protests increased, the draft system became harder to operate. By early 1969, states had backlogs of thousands of cases against people who had failed to report for duty after being drafted. In San Francisco alone, more than 100 attorneys offered free legal services to men trying to beat the draft. There were several ways to do this. One possible route was to claim that one suffered from physical or mental ill-health and to find a sympathetic doctor with antiwar views who would agree. Men who had contacts or sufficient money often fled to Canada, where they were beyond the reach of the draft. Again, such means of avoiding military service tended to be more available to the better-educated and the better-off.

One way out of the draft was to apply to be classed as a conscientious objector. Pacifists had first been allowed to avoid military service by a law passed in 1940. But as more people applied to be classed as conscientious objectors to beat the Vietnam

KEY THEMES

The Gates Commission

Richard M. Nixon promised in the 1968 presidential campaign to end the draft if he was elected. Nixon wanted to create an all-volunteer army. He believed that ending the draft would stop many protests against the war. Facing opposition from the Department of Defense, he asked Thomas S. Gates, Jr, to look into the all-volunteer idea. In February 1970, Gates's commission reported that military strength could be maintained without conscription. With troops still needed in Vietnam, it was not until early 1973 that the end of draft orders was announced.

▲ Members of the Joint Chiefs of Staff pose in 1964. They were the heads of the U.S. military services.

▲ Students burn a draft card in Washington, D.C., in June 1968. The act could lead to a heavy fine or imprisonment.

draft, the criteria were tightened up. In 1965, the U.S. Supreme Court ruled that, to qualify as a conscientious objector, an applicant had to show evidence that his commitment to pacifism was as strong as, and shaped his life in the same way as, a religious belief in God.

Although the major churches argued that opposition to a war was a question of individual conscience and should merit exemption from the draft, the courts rejected this argument. The courts ruled that opposition to the Vietnam War was generally politically motivated rather than being based on religious belief. But despite the strict criteria for eligibility, the number of conscientious objectors increased from 17,900 in 1964 to 61,000 in 1971.

End of the draft

When, in 1969, Yale University President Kingman Brewster told the graduating class that the draft made a mockery of service to the nation, the end of the draft was near. The government set up the Gates Commission to determine its future. The commission issued its findings in 1970, making it clear that the draft was no longer relevant. In 1973 the All-Volunteer Force replaced all forms of conscripted military service.

Chapter 2

Antiwar Movement

From 1965, the growing scale of the war in Vietnam was matched by mounting protests at home.

Protests against the war at home became increasingly strong as the conflict went on. The protests influenced not only government policy but also the whole timescale of the war itself. The antiwar movement expanded from being a student-led protest to a national movement in a matter of months during 1965, the year the United States officially entered the war.

The first marches

The first protests against the war were often led by civil-rights organizations. In April 1965, Students for a Democratic Society, led by Tom Hayden, mobilized 25,000 people to march on Washington, D.C. The march was held to protest against growing U.S. involvement in Vietnam. Despite such a demonstration, however, opinion polls suggested that the war was actually

▲ A demonstrator holds up one of the most popular antiwar slogans during a protest by 50,000 people in Washington, D.C., on October 21, 1967.

becoming more popular. At the start of 1965, a poll had shown that only about 40 percent of Americans supported the policy of Lyndon B. Johnson's government of becoming more involved in Vietnam. Despite protests during the spring, that number actually rose. By the summer, two-thirds of Americans said that they backed the government's approach.

A minority activity

Even at the end of 1965, protest remained limited to a minority of people. It was led largely by student organizations. There were a number of reasons for this. Firstly, young students came from the generation who were likely to have to go to war. That made them question more than others why the country was fighting. A civil war 8,000 miles away did not seem a sufficient reason for U.S. military

involvement. Right from the start, many of those in line for military service found ways to avoid it. Even parents who had approved of the draft and who supported the idea of the war in Vietnam often helped their sons avoid the draft.

Tradition of protest

Students also took the lead because they had a tradition of civil protests. Until 1965, college campuses had been leading centers of the civil rights struggle. With the passage of the Voting Rights Act in 1965, which banned any discriminatory voting practices that had kept the vote from African Americans for so long, the civil rights protesters felt they had won the first round in the civil rights battle. But involvement in the movement had given many students the idea that it was their duty

▼ Vietnam veterans stage an antiwar rally in Washington, D.C., in May 1967.

KEY THEMES

Anchorman

The CBS anchorman, Walter Cronkite, was one of America's most popular and trusted figures. After the assault on the U.S. Embassy in Saigon on January 31, 1968, Cronkite went to Vietnam to see for himself what was going on. On February 27, 1968, he made a rare personal report, saying that it was "more certain than ever that the bloody experience of Vietnam is to end in stalemate." His comments had a profound effect. It was clear that public support for the war was gone and that a negotiated settlement was the only way out.

to take a stand against injustice. Because many of them believed that U.S. involvement in Vietnam was morally wrong, they began to focus on bringing the conflict to an end.

Variety of tactics

The civil rights struggle meant that young Americans knew that protest could be effective. Antiwar activists tried a range of tactics. In June 1965, activists tried to halt troop trains by holding up the 173d Airborne Brigade, which was on its way to Saigon. Later that summer, the Vietnam Day Committee, formed on the campus of the University of California at Berkeley earlier in the year, organized further attempts to stop

▼ Guards cordon off the Pentagon in Washington, D.C., during the huge antiwar demonstration of October 21, 1967.

trains. They were unsuccessful. Only a few hard-core radicals were actually prepared to stand in front of a train full of armed troops. Most protestors just picketed induction centers or march in demonstrations.

Burning draft cards became another means of protest. In mid-October 1965, David Millar, a 22-year-old Jesuit charity worker in a Bowery soup kitchen, held up his draft card at an antiwar rally in New York City. "I believe the napalming of villages is

KEY PERSONALITY

Norman Mailer

The U.S. novelist Norman Mailer had many macho attitudes toward fighting, but he was pessimistic about the war in Vietnam. In 1967 he published a novel, Why Are We in Vietnam?, which he bizarrely set in Alaska rather than Vietnam. His 1968 novel The Armies of the Night was based on his experience at an antiwar demonstration in Washington, D.C. Mailer hoped to persuade people that the war was wrong. But he was preaching to the converted. The people who supported the war—blue-collar workers and middle America— rarely read his work.

▲ A protestor wears antiradiation clothing during a student demonstration against the war in November 1968.

17

an immoral act," he declared, holding a match to the corner of his card. "I hope this is a significant act—so here goes." Millar lit the card and, at the end of that month, became the first man to be charged under a new law that made draft-card burning a federal offense with a maximum penalty of five years in jail and a $10,000 fine. Millar's act became an often-repeated means of protest. The nightly TV news regularly featured draftees burning their draft cards. The cameras would also capture furious onlookers attacking the protestors or attempting to extinguish the flames with water or fire extinguishers.

Momentum gathers

The antiwar protests were gathering momentum, however. On November 27, 1965, some 30,000 demonstrators marched

▼ A banner at a demonstration in November 1969 links the war on Vietnam to the "war" on black Americans.

KEY THEMES

The Pentagon Papers

In June 1967, at the request of the Secretary of Defense, Robert McNamara, 36 defense analysts reviewed U.S. policy in Vietnam. The report took 18 months to compile and ran to 7,100 pages. Because it criticized U.S. policy, the government only printed 15 copies. An analyst secretly passed the report to Senator William Fulbright, chairman of the Senate Foreign Relations Committee, and to The New York Times, which published part of it on June 13, 1971. President Nixon tried to stop newspapers from publishing the study but the Supreme Court quashed his injunctions and criticized his attempts to silence the press.

through Washington, D.C. The protest was organized by SANE, the Committee for a Sane Nuclear Policy, which counted the child-rearing guru of the 1960s, Dr Benjamin Spock, as its most famous member. Spock's presence at the rally was an important boost to the antiwar movement's respectability in the eyes of the public and attracted many other older liberals. As the protestors marched around the White House, their moderate banners called for a "Supervised Ceasefire" and claimed that "War Erodes the Great Society."

President Johnson issued a statement the following day saying that "Dissent is a sign of political vigor." The real vigor in the debate, however, came not from the liberals outside the White House but from the radical antiwar protesters across the country who were burning their draft cards. Clashes between antiwar demonstrators and those who supported the war became a feature of daily life.

Antiwar protestors

In New York and Chicago students seized and occupied university buildings. At New York University, 130 students and members of the faculty walked out when Secretary of Defense, Robert McNamara, arrived to collect an honorary degree. By 1967, the war had split American society.

Antiwar intellectuals such as the novelist Norman Mailer and the linguistics professor

◀ Students like these, protesting at Howard University in October 1969, often had a background in the civil rights movement.

▶ Antiwar protestors face the bayonets of National Guard wearing gasmasks at a protest in October 1967.

Vietnam Veterans against the War

In April 1967 six servicemen who had returned from Vietnam met on an antiwar march in Washington, D.C. They founded Vietnam Veterans Against the War (VVAW) to represent men and women who had been in Vietnam who believed the war should be ended. VVAW events were relatively small, including a two-day occupation of the Statue of Liberty at Christmas 1971. But the fact that they had fought overseas helped them attract a lot of publicity for the antiwar cause.

Noam Chomsky addressed college "teach-ins" organized by Students for a Democratic Society. In 1967, antiwar intellectuals started to appear on television. Guests openly expressed their opposition to the war on the popular late-night talk show, *Johnny Carson's Tonight*, although Carson was careful to keep his opinion to himself.

More protests followed. On the weekend of April 15–16, 1967, 125,000 antiwar demonstrators gathered in New York. In Central Park, protestors carried placards that said "Draft beer, not boys." On October 21, 1967, around 50,000 demonstrators marched on the Pentagon in Washington, D.C. In a

▲ **Demonstrators carry a model bomb during an antiwar march. For many Americans, the idea of indiscriminate bombing of nations with few air defenses was highly immoral.**

President Johnson remarked, "If I've lost Walter, I've lost Mr. Average Citizen." Johnson did not stand for re-election.

Further protests

When it became clear that Johnson's successor, Richard Nixon, was sending more troops to the war, protests at home strenghtened. In September 1969, Sam Brown formed the Vietnam Moratorium Committee to show that antiwar protestors were not just students. On October 15, 1969, the committee mobilized 250,000 people to march in Washington, D.C. Meanwhile, as SDS grew more militant, violence escalated. One SDS faction, the Weather Underground, planted more than 5,000 bombs.

televised showdown, they faced 10,000 U.S. Army troops and National Guardsmen armed with rifles but no ammunition. The demonstration began peacefully but descended into violence. Norman Mailer described the event in his 1968 antiwar novel *The Armies of the Night*.

The key moment of the antiwar protests came in May 1970. The Ohio National Guard opened fire on a student protest at Kent State University, killing four students. Americans were horrified. Although Nixon dismissed the protestors as "bums," he was forced to withdraw U.S. troops from Cambodia, and Congress cut funding for the war. The protests continued. In November 1971, there were large-scale rallies in 16 U.S. cities. A poll showed that 73 percent of Americans wanted the war ended. By now the government had opened the peace talks that led to the end of the war just over a year later, in January 1973.

A turning point

A major turning point came with the 1968 Tet Offensive. America was humiliated as Communists temporarily occupied the U.S. Embassy in Saigon, and support for the war evaporated. Tet even convinced the popular CBS newsreader Walter Cronkite that the war was a mistake. When he said so on TV,

Chapter 3

Public Opinion and Politics

The growth of opposition to the war in Vietnam had a profound impact on domestic politics in the United States.

The Vietnam War began against a backdrop of great political change in the United States. After World War II, during which 2.5 million African American men had registered for the draft between 1941 and 1945, and some 50,000 had seen combat, the idea of racial segregation had started to seem inappropriate and out of date. By the late 1950s and early 1960s the civil rights movement was growing across the country's campuses and with the civil rights movement came an increased political awareness and belief in the right to challenge the accepted ideas of the day.

▲ The Democratic Majority Leader in Congress, Lyndon B. Johnson (left), became president in 1963.

The war and race

Many of the civil rights leaders were committed pacifists. Martin Luther King, Jr., spoke out against the war, for example. King commanded great moral authority and his opinion was closely listened to. The Vietnam war itself was racially divisive. For most African American youths it was not as easy to avoid the draft as it was for their middle-class white contemporaries. President

▲ Pacifists demonstrate outside the White House in November 1965. The unpopularity of the war was growing during Johnson's presidency.

Lyndon B. Johnson deliberately introduced a policy that drafted African Americans before white Americans. He did this because he felt that having African Americans in the armed services would give him the chance to provide them with improved health care and education opportunities and help to promote their social advancement.

For many African Americans this was initially acceptable. They saw fighting for their country as a chance to show how much they contributed to society. Others thought that the war in Vietnam had nothing to do with them and that the real enemy—those who approved of segregation in U.S. society—was not in Vietnam. They were back at home.

Public opinion began to turn against the war when statistics revealed that African Americans were more likely to die or be injured than their white counterparts. In 1965, eight percent of U.S. military personnel in Vietnam were black, but African Americans made up some 23 percent of the enlisted soldiers killed in action. The growing feeling was that African Americans were being unfairly sacrificed. Rioting against the war broke out in the black ghettos of northern U.S. cities and the West Coast.

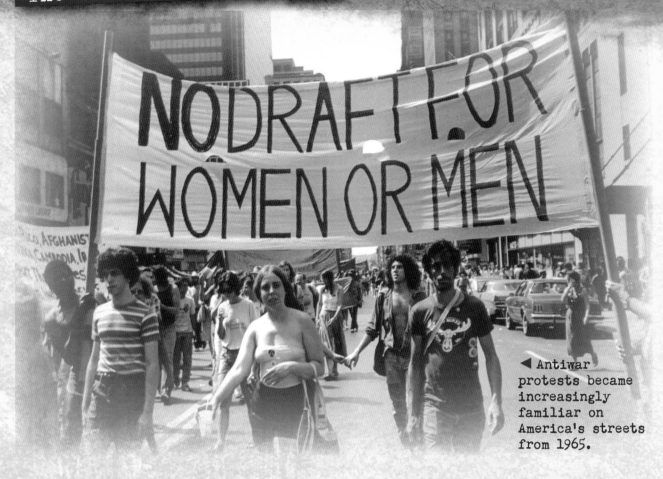

◄ Antiwar protests became increasingly familiar on America's streets from 1965.

Divided opinion

Across the country, public opinion was split. Clashes between antiwar demonstrators and those who supported the war became commonplace. The leading ranks of a New York march were covered with red paint, and in Chicago and Oakland demonstrators were pelted with eggs.

By 1967, U.S. society was divided on broad lines. The educated and those on the left-wing tended to be against the war, while blue-collar workers and those living in the middle of the country tended to support it. Some Americans began to fear that their country was becoming ungovernable,

especially after TV coverage showed African Americans rioting against the war. By 1967, the mounting casualties in Vietnam after two years of hard fighting were beginning to persuade the general public that the war would prove unwinnable.

Although most people still condemned the antiwar protestors, the demonstrations started to have a political effect. Senior politicians such as William J. Fulbright, the Chairman of the Senate Foreign Relations Committee, Senator Robert Kennedy, and Senator Eugene McCarthy expressed their doubts about the war. President Johnson held firm but his Secretary of Defense,

Robert McNamara, who had been the chief architect of the war, began to turn against it. In addition, the commander on the ground in Vietnam, General William Westmoreland, said the war could not be won without a massive increase in the number of troops. This would involve extending the already unpopular draft. With the rioting in the streets, it was clear that the country would not stand for more troops being sent.

New president

Events in Vietnam proved decisive in shaping the outcome of the 1968 presidential election. Following America's humiliation during the January Tet Offensive, President Johnson announced he would not run for another term

► Reporters crowd around William Averell Harriman (center), U.S. delegate to the peace talks in Paris, in October 1968.

KEY THEMES

Primary Surprise

In 1968, Lyndon B. Johnson did not contest the primaries to be the Democrats' presidential candidate; he assumed he would win. His opponent was the antiwar Senator Eugene McCarthy of Minnesota. The Johnson team said a McCarthy victory would be "greeted with cheers in Hanoi." On March 12, New Hampshire voters gave McCarthy 40 percent of the vote. A shocked Johnson decided not to stand for re-election.

in office. Senator Eugene McCarthy, who was virtually unknown, was running as a peace candidate. He had already taken 42 percent of the poll in the New Hampshire Democratic primary. Four days later, Senator Robert Kennedy entered the Democratic race, also on an antiwar ticket. He was assassinated in June 1968 before he could secure the party's presidential nomination.

The Democratic Party convention in Chicago in August 1968 turned into a full-scale riot. Hubert Humphrey, as expected, won the party's nomination to run against Richard Nixon in the presidential election, but Humphrey was already tarnished with his support for a prowar policy.

Nixon was elected on a promise to end the war. However, when it became clear that he

◀ The U.S. Marines' resistance to the siege at Khe Sanh in early 1968 was a major morale boost to the United States.

was escalating the war rather than winding it down in 1969, public opinion grew even more hostile. The number of protestors grew and demonstrations became a regular occurrence. As many as a quarter of a million Americans marched on Washington D.C. on October 15, 1969.

Nixon gives in

In May 1970, four college students were killed when the Ohio National Guard opened fire during protests at Kent State University. Public outrage caused Nixon to change his policy in Vietnam. Nixon had originally dismissed the actions of

▼ A pitched battle erupts between protestors and police in Chicago on the night of August 28, 1968.

KEY MOMENT
- -
Chicago Convention Riots

The 1968 Democratic Convention held in August in Chicago turned into a full-scale riot. Even before the convention opened, it was clear that there would be trouble. The National Guard was put on standby and given orders to kill if necessary. A wide range of antiwar protestors flooded into the hot, humid city. Antiwar and pro-government delegates clashed daily inside the hall, while outside the police fought with protestors and fired tear gas at them. The events were broadcast daily to a shocked public. For the Democrats, in particular, the convention was a disaster. It left scars that have still not healed today.

▶ Richard Nixon salutes a crowd on the presidential campaign trail in 1968.

the students, calling them bums and saying, "When dissent turns to violence, it invites tragedy." But he was nevertheless forced to withdraw troops from Cambodia, where they had been conducting a large-scale covert operation. People would not tolerate seeing young Americans gunned down for exercising their constitutional right to free speech and free assembly.

Congress forced Nixon to promise that U.S. troops would push no deeper into Cambodia than 21 miles (33 km) from the border and would withdraw completely in a matter of weeks. Congress also sought to limit the president's powers. It repealed the Gulf of Tonkin Resolution of 1964, which had given the president the power to conduct

the conflict in Southeast Asia. Nixon was not concerned. He thought his power to act in Southeast Asia rested on his authority as commander-in-chief and not as president.

The Pentagon Papers

As promised, Nixon withdrew U.S. troops from Cambodia, but he continued the illegal bombing. The lies and secrets would become a matter of public interest in 1971 when *The*

▼ A man burns his draft card at an antiwar demonstration in Central Park, New York City, in April 1967.

New York Times and other newspapers, including *The Washington Post*, published extracts from the so-called Pentagon Papers. This was a secret government report that documented years of U.S. government deception and incompetence in Vietnam. The public was appalled. To make matters worse, Nixon used injunctions to try to stop the press publishing the report. When a Supreme Court ruling of June 30 quashed the injunctions, criticizing his attempts to stop the freedom of the press, the reputation of the presidential office and the government sank still lower. Many Americans asked themselves how the country could have sunk so low as to not only send young men to their deaths in Vietnam but also to lie repeatedly to its people.

Continuing protests

Protests continued. In May 1971, 12,000 demonstrators were arrested in Washington, D.C. Opinion polls now showed that the vast majority of Americans wanted the war to end immediately. Nixon sent his National Security Advisor, Henry Kissinger, to begin peace talks with the Vietnamese in Paris, France. The negotiations were long—the North Vietnamese believed that, if they waited, public opinion would force the United States to simply stop fighting. But after the United States bombed North Vietnam to force it to continue negotiating, a settlement was reached in November 1972. The Peace Accord was signed the following January.

Chapter 4

The Cost of the War

The conflict was costly both financially and in its physical and emotional impact on individuals, families, and whole societies.

Both sides paid an extremely high price for the Vietnam War in terms not just of the financial cost of the conflict, which was huge, but also in terms of personal cost. Many people in both North and South Vietnam and in the United States lost a family member to death or injury. Some individuals are still paying the cost of the war today, as Vietnam veterans continue to struggle with long-term physical and psychological damage.

◀ A U.S. tank makes a patrol in August 1969. The cost of the military hardware sent to Vietnam for both U.S. and South Vietnamese forces was huge.

▲ Signals and medical staff arrive in South Vietnam in 1965; vast amounts of U.S. military aid were poured into the country.

The war also made an impact on the life of whole nations. South Vietnam ceased to exist, and many South Vietnamese found it difficult to live in a Communist society. The United States was profoundly affected by its involvement in Vietnam and its ultimate defeat. Public faith in the government and trust in political leaders was badly shaken. The belief that the United States must intervene to solve the world's troubles—a belief that had shaped U.S. foreign policy since the 1940s—was undermined. The war and the way in which it was fought gave Americans no choice but to face up to the complex moral decisions involved in warfare. This was no simple fight between right and wrong. In early 21st-century wars waged against terrorist groups in Afghanistan and Iraq, many Americans urged their leaders to

◀ A barge carries U.S. M48 Patton tanks to a base at Long Binh. Such hardware was often of limited use in the Vietnamese landscape.

remember what had happened in Vietnam before they committed the military to what were seen by many to be unwinnable wars.

Shock statistics

The statistics for the Vietnam War are shocking. More than two million Americans served in the conflict. Of the 1.6 million who faced combat, more than 58,000 were killed and a further 300,000 were physically wounded. Many more were psychologically damaged, but that fact was not generally recognized for many years after the war ended. More Vietnam veterans committed suicide after the conflict than died during it. Another 2,387 Americans were listed as "missing in action."

Losses on the Vietnamese side were even bigger. Vietnam did not release an official estimate of the numbers killed until 1995. As many as two million civilians in both North and South Vietnam were killed during the war. Among the Viet Cong (VC) and North Vietnamese Army (NVA), military casualties were 1.1 million dead and wounded. The United States had estimated the number of casualties in the South Vietnamese Army (ARVN) to be between 200,000 and 250,000 soldiers. Other nations fought in the war for South Vietnam and suffered casualties: South Korea lost more than 4,000 dead, Thailand around 350, Australia more than 500, and New Zealand around 36.

Environmental impact

Vietnam, along with neighboring Laos and Cambodia, also suffered lasting environmental damage in the war, mainly from the spraying of chemicals by U.S. airplanes. During the war, defoliants were sprayed from the air.

KEY THEMES

Communist Casualties

Over nearly 30 years of conflict, the North Vietnamese Army (NVA) grew from a small insurgency force into one of the world's largest armed forces. The original fighting in South Vietnam was waged by the Viet Cong, but the NVA was forced to commit more and more units, particularly after the 1968 Tet Offensive, which resulted in Viet Cong casualties of about 45,000 dead. The NVA's great strength was its resources of manpower, and its ability to absorb high casualties. According to Vietnamese government figures released in 1995, as many as 1,100,000 NVA and Viet Cong were killed during the conflict.

These chemicals caused the leaves to fall off trees in order that the enemy would no longer be able to hide in the dense foliage. Without the jungle canopy, the Americans believed, the NVA and VC would be easier to spot. In fact, the tactic was a double-edged sword. Areas that had been defoliated left no cover for U.S. soldiers as they moved around.

Aerial spraying began in 1961, at the request of South Vietnam's President Diem. U.S. officials were concerned that use of chemical weapons might breach the 1925 Geneva Protocol, which laid out international rules on chemical warfare. President John F.

▶ A young Vietnamese girl grieves at the funeral of her father, killed by Communists while fighting for the Army of the South Vietnam (ARVN) in 1968.

New Arrivals

Many Southern Vietnamese immigrated to the United States. Early migrants were unpopular, but the Refugee Act of 1980 relaxed restrictions on entry. Between 1981 and 2000, 531,310 refugees arrived from Vietnam. Voluntary organizations provided them with food, clothing, and shelter. The new arrivals were spread around, so that no city was overburdened, but many later formed large communities. Today, around 40 percent of all Vietnamese Americans live in Orange County, California.

▲ Bombs are loaded on a B-52. Each B-52 mission cost about $30,000; in 1967 there were some 600 sorties a month.

Kennedy approved the use of herbicides on the grounds that they were widely used at home. By November 1962, aerial spraying was widespread.

By the time the spraying program ended in 1971, 18 million gallons of chemicals had been dropped. Some 20 percent of Vietnam's jungle—6 million acres (2.4 million hectares)—had been razed.

The chemicals did not only affect vegetation. Observers soon noticed that the spraying caused respiratory problems in Vietnamese children and in U.S. soldiers working in the affected areas. In 1969, it was discovered that one of the chemicals used, Agent Orange, contained dioxin, which caused cancer and birth defects.

The same year, the use of dioxins was banned by the United Nations. In 1975, President Ford banned the use of herbicides in war. Vietnam veterans filed 32,000 disability claims over the use of Agent Orange and many Vietnamese have reported birth defects since the end of the war.

As well as destroying much of Vietnam's jungle, U.S. bombing destroyed agriculture, business, and industrial infrastructure. Large parts of the countryside were left littered with land mines. Analysts put the weight of bombs dropped on both North and South Vietnam at over five million tonnes (4.9 t). In neighboring Laos, more bombs were dropped per head of population than had ever happened anywhere. U.S. aircraft flew 580,000 bombing missions over Laos, and more than 30 percent of the bombs remained unexploded after the war ended. Even today, old bombs still maim people.

▼ **Australian troops hold a memorial service for colleagues who died in the Battle of Long Thanh in 1966.**

Financial costs

In June 1974, the Department of Defense estimated that the cost of the Vietnam War had been $145 billion. But there were also unmeasured costs, such as inflation caused by the war economy, lost production, interest on loans, and continuing benefits paid to the veterans. The real cost of the war might have been nearer $300 billion: over $1,000 for every American man, woman, and child.

Shells cost around $100 each. At the height of the war, 10,000 shells were dropped each day. Eight million tons of bombs were dropped on Vietnam, Laos, and Cambodia, or three times the weight of bombs dropped on Germany in World War II. During 1966 alone, 148,000 missions were flown over North Vietnam at a cost of $1.25 billion, causing

▶ A 10-year-old Vietnamese boy comforts his younger sister after both had been left orphaned by fighting at Bien Hoa.

KEY THEMES

. . . .

Missing in Action

The fate of soldiers listed as "missing in action" (MIA) was unknown even after the war. Up to 1,350 MIA may have been held as prisoners of war (POWs). A lack of accurate information made it impossible to verify numbers. At the end of the war, Operation Homecoming brought home 591 MIA who had been held prisoner. But many Americans believed that MIA were still being held in remote parts of Vietnam.

$130 million of damage. In other words, every dollar's worth of damage the United States inflicted cost it $9.60.

For the Vietnamese, the costs were also high. Between 1965 and 1971, North Vietnam's defense budget was $3.56 billion. The Soviet Union contributed a further $1.66 billion and the Chinese $670 million. That gave the Communists a total of $5.89 billion, a fraction of the spending of the United States and its South Vietnamese allies.

Damaged reputation

After defeat in Vietnam, the U.S. military remained discredited for years. It eventually rebuilt its reputation, but since Vietnam the U.S. public has been more wary of calls to intervene abroad. The Democratic majority

Prisoners of War

The 1949 Geneva Convention sets out rules for the humane treatment of prisoners of war (POWs). In Vietnam, the rules often did not apply. Between 1968 and 1972, U.S. POWs were detained in North Vietnam in 13 permanent detention camps. Most of them were based around the capital, Hanoi, including the infamous Hoa Lo detention center. It was better known by its ironic nickname, the "Hanoi Hilton." Many U.S. prisoners were tortured and interrogated there, including John McCain, later a U.S. Senator.

in Congress enacted the 1973 War Powers Resolution, which limited the power of the President to send U.S. troops into combat. Congress was eager to set limits on U.S. power across the globe and to limit the costs Americans would pay for foreign policy. In the next 25 years, the public expressed unease at a U.S. military presence in places as far apart as Bosnia and Nicaragua.

In a newly unified Vietnam, the military who had served the South were treated harshly. The dead were not acknowledged or honored. Those who survived found it hard to get jobs. In part this may reflect the fact that Vietnam is a young country: some 60 percent of the Vietnamese population has been born since 1973 and has little time for the war.

▶ Wounded soldiers wait on a U.S. Navy ship to be sent home to the United States.

Chapter 5

The Veterans

A generation of U.S. servicemen and women had their lives changed by the conflict in Vietnam.

For the ordinary soldier in Vietnam, the war was a devastating and life-changing experience. As the conflict dragged on with no end in sight, draftees became increasingly unwilling to serve. Casualties were growing and the troops were receiving an unprecedented bad press back home. Rather than being seen as heroes, draftees and the volunteers of the regular U.S. Army were tainted by their participation in an unpopular war. Many frontline troops came to believe that they were being asked to lay down their lives for a cause that few back home believed in.

Many troops also had little faith in their generals and political leaders. None of these senior people seemed to have any clear idea about how to bring the war to a successful conclusion. News of the massacre of South Vietnamese peasants by U.S. troops at My Lai in 1969 was revealed in 1970. Details of the atrocity added to the antiwar sentiment that was sweeping the United States. The stage was set for a difficult homecoming for those who had served in Vietnam.

▲ Frederick Hart sculpted "The Three Soldiers," at the Vietnam Veterans' Memorial in Washington, D.C., in 1984.

A bitter defeat

The United States had never lost a war before Vietnam. For many Americans, what made the defeat even harder to stand was that U.S. soldiers never lost a single battle in Vietnam and yet still lost the war. The argument went that, if the military had not been defeated in Vietnam, then the loss of the war must somehow be due to a wider failure of politics and national morale.

It was clear that U.S. foreign policy had been misguided. For the first time in American history, Americans were forced to look at themselves and their society and re-evaluate both. Before the war, the idea that America was the greatest nation on Earth had been alive and well. Americans saw

▼ Former ARVN soldiers in Detroit, Michigan, meet in 2010 to mark 30 years since the fall of Saigon.

themselves as the nation that had saved the world from a bitter world war and preserved democracy. After Vietnam, America faced a new reality. Not only had the war been lost. Its leaders had lied; some of its soldiers had committed appalling atrocities; and U.S. society had almost fallen apart. That was the reality to which Vietnam veterans returned.

Bittersweet homecoming

During the 1970s, the most remarkable thing about the Vietnam War became the speed with which most Americans forgot about it.

▲ Flowers are left as a tribute at the Vietnam Veterans' Memorial Wall, designed by the U.S. architect Maya Lin in 1982; the wall lists 58,195 names of the dead.

Many people did not talk about it; instead, they ignored it and almost pretended it had never happened. Most Americans wanted life to go back to "normal." As a result, Vietnam became the "forgotten war"—and its veterans became forgotten soldiers. They were unwelcome reminders of a time most people would sooner forget.

Unlike the veterans of wars that marked the new millennium in Iraq and Afghanistan, Vietnam veterans returned home without ceremony. There was no debrief or official process for becoming readjusted to normal life. Some soldiers flew home alone and were back with their families only 40 hours after leaving the front line.

Even the one million soldiers who had only served one-year tours had seen more fighting than most veterans of World War II. On their return to America, they were rushed back into daily life without any chance to process their traumatic experiences. They said goodbye to their fellow soldiers and combat units and were back among those who, while glad to have them home, did not want to know about the horrors they had seen. The rejection of the Vietnam veterans was made all the worse because many could remember the triumphant return of their fathers after World War II.

The Vietnam Veterans had few support groups. Most were young—the average age was 19—and most had seen friends die and witnessed appalling destruction that had fundamentally changed them. Many veterans, realizing that they were unlikely to receive sympathy, did not talk about their problems. Instead, they dealt with the trauma of war in a self-harming and destructive way. Drink and drug abuse became common.

Withdrawal from society

Many veterans were in pain, had lost limbs, or suffered nightmares. As many as 850,000 were suffering from what would now be recognized as

Post-traumatic Stress Disorder. Their condition was not addressed and dealt with until 20 years after the war ended. The government and the Veterans Administration (now the Department of Veterans' Affairs) refused to admit that veterans were suffering from any postwar problems until recurring issues were recorded among Vietnam veterans in the mid-1980s.

The 1980s saw a change in attitude toward the veterans. In 1978, a group of veterans

▶ This monument, created by Glenna Goodacre in 1993, honors some 7,500 women who served in Vietnam, mainly as nurses.

formed the organization Vietnam Veterans of America (VVA). Their founding principle was "Never again will one generation of veterans abandon another." They were instrumental in lobbying for better care and recognition of the on-going sacrifice made by those who had served in the war. Today, the VVA membership stands at over 65,000.

Changing attitudes

Hollywood also started to take an interest in the war during the late 1970s and 1980s. A number of movies appeared that dealt not only with the horrors of the war itself, but also with the difficult homecoming. *The Deer Hunter* (1978) told the story of three Russian American steelworker buddies and their time in Vietnam. It shows the trauma of the war and the survivors' homecoming. The film was a critical and box-office hit, winning five Oscars.

The Deer Hunter was followed in 1979 by *Apocalypse Now*. It was an epic movie that made the war the backdrop for a personal journey into a hellish world. It suggested

KEY PERSONALITY

John McCain

The son of a four-star general, John McCain volunteered for combat duty as a Navy pilot in Vietnam. On October 23, 1967, he was shot down over Hanoi. When the North Vietnamese offered to release him, McCain refused. He served five and a half years at the infamous "Hanoi Hilton," where he was tortured and beaten. He was released in March 1973 and began a career in politics. In 2008, he was the Republican candidate for president, but was defeated by Barack Obama.

◀ Ron Kovic answers a question in 1974, during a hunger strike by veterans against conditions in veterans' hospitals.

the psychological stress that jungle warfare against an unseen enemy could create, and how it could make anyone a little crazy.

From being ignored, the Vietnam War was now the subject of major movies. Many more would follow throughout the 1980s, including *Platoon* (1986), based on the director Oliver Stone's own experiences in Vietnam, and *Full Metal Jacket* (1987).

Government attitudes

A series of U.S. administrations realized that the government needed to acknowledge the sacrifice made by those who had served in

KEY PERSONALITY
Ron Kovic

Ron Kovic was paralyzed when he was shot in Vietnam. He was treated in the Bronx Veterans Hospital, where the dirty conditions infuriated him. Kovic burst onto the national stage as an antiwar campaigner when he disrupted Richard M. Nixon's speech at the Republican National Convention in 1972. His memoir, *Born on the Fourth of July*, was turned into a successful movie.

► A young relative of a Vietnam veteran attends a rally in support of veterans in Washington, D.C., in 2004.

Vietnam. In 1979 the veteran Jan Scruggs formed the Vietnam Veterans Memorial Fund (VVMF). He lobbied Congress for a two-acre plot of land in the Constitution Gardens in Washington, D.C., to create a suitable memorial.

President Jimmy Carter signed legislation the following year to create a memorial. Maya Ying Lin, at the time a Chinese American student at Yale, won the architectural competition to design a memorial. Her winning design was a simple but elegant black polished granite wall that blends into the surrounding gardens. On it are inscribed the names of every American to die in the war in the order of their deaths. To date, 58,267 names have been inscribed. The list is continually updated as remains of missing soldiers are still being found or identified. The memorial wall was completed in 1984. Its dedication marked a complete reversal in the way the Vietnam veterans are now viewed in wider society.

Over the decades since the end of the Vietnam War, Americans have come to understand the conflict better and

▼ As a young man, the Democratic politician Al Gore enlisted to go to Vietnam, although few of his Harvard classmates served.

to recognize the sacrifice of those who were sent there. Similarly, in Vietnam, the perception of the war is slowly changing. There, however, the process has been slower. The Communist government withheld information about the war for many years after the fighting finished, and those who fought for South Vietnam were seen as criminals. Many were imprisoned or even executed; many more left Vietnam. It was only from the 1990s on that the Vietnamese government has been more open about the war and the experiences of the veterans.

GLOSSARY

assassination A murder carried out for political reasons.

atrocity A crime of great or horrific violence carried out in wartime.

civil rights The movement to gain voting and other rights for black Americans in the late 1950s and early 1960s.

Cold War An ideological conflict between the United States and its allies on one hand and the Soviet Union and Communist countries on the other; the Cold War lasted from 1946 untli 1989.

conscientious objector Someone whose beliefs do not allow them to inflict violence, and therefore to fight in a war.

deferment The official postponment of military service.

defoliant A chemical designed to kill plants or cause them to lose their leaves.

deployment The distribution of military forces ready for action.

draft Compulsory enrolment in the military services.

draftee Someone who has been forced to join the military services.

escalation An increase in size or scope.

inflation A general rise in prices.

militant Following an aggressive course of action.

morale The fighting spirit of an individual or a group, and how much they believe in victory.

napalm A jelly like substance used in bombs designed to stick to people and ignite.

post-traumatic stress disorder A psychological reaction that occurs after a highly stressful experience, usually with nightmares and other flashbacks.

radical Holding extreme viewpoints or supporting extreme action.

segregation To separate sections of society on the basis of race, religion, etc.

stalemate A contest in which neither side can win but neither can be defeated.

FURTHER RESOURCES

Books

Burrows, J.S. *The Vietnam War Memorial* (War Memorials). Rourke Publishing Group, 2009.

Gitlin, Marty. *U.S. Involvement in Vietnam* (Essential Events). Abdo Publishing Company, 2010.

Kent, Deborah. *The Vietnam War: From Da Nang to Saigon* (The United States at War). Enslow Publishing Inc, 2011.

Koestler-Grack, Rachel A. *The Kent State Tragedy* (American Moments). Abdo Publishing Company, 2005.

McNeese, Tim. *The Cold War and Postwar America, 1946–1963*. Chelsea House Publications, 2010.

O'Connell, Kim A. *Primary Source Accounts of the Vietnam War* (America's Wars through Primary Sources). Myreportlinks.com, 2006.

The Vietnam War (Perspectives on Modern World History). Greenhaven Press, 2011.

Wiest, Andrew. *The Vietnam War* (Essential Histories: War and Conflict in Modern Times). Rosen Publishing Group, 2008.

Young, Marilyn A., John J. Fitzgerald, and A. Tom Grunfeld. *The Vietnam War: A History in Documents* (Pages from History). Oxford University Press, USA, 2002.

Websites

http://www.pbs.org/wgbh/amex/vietnam/
Online companion to the PBS series *Vietnam: A Television History*.

www.history.com/topics/vietnam-war
History.com page of links about the Vietnam War.

http://www.spartacus.schoolnet.co.uk/vietnam.htm
Spartacus Educational page with links to biographies and other articles.

INDEX